Background

Tax return preparers serve a critical role in tax administration and represent an important intermediary between taxpayers and the Internal Revenue Service (IRS). The IRS processed about 77 million individual electronically filed (e-filed) Federal income tax returns prepared by paid tax return preparers in Calendar Year (CY) 2013. Figure 1 shows the most common types and number of return preparers as of January 3, 2014.

Figure 1: Types and Number of Paid Tax Return Preparers

Unenrolled or Unlicensed Tax Return Preparers	Number
These tax return preparers range from those who might receive extensive training to those with little or no training. Currently, only four States (California, Maryland, New York, and Oregon) have requirements such as registration and continuing education requirements for unenrolled paid tax return preparers.	403,008
Tax Return Preparers With Professional Credentials	
Licensed professionals, such as attorneys and certified public accountants, are regulated by the State licensing authority and related associations such as the American Bar Association and the American Institute of Certified Public Accountants.	256,669
Enrolled agents are professionals who pass an IRS examination or present evidence of qualifying experience as a former IRS employee and have been issued an enrollment card. Enrolled agents are the only taxpayer representatives who receive their right to represent clients in matters that involve the IRS from the Federal Government.	51,879

Source: IRS Return Preparer Office (RPO).

Because of the critical role they have in helping taxpayers to comply with the tax laws, identifying problem preparers through the complaint process is an essential component of the IRS's oversight responsibilities. Unqualified or unethical tax return preparers can negatively impact taxpayers as well as tax revenue if the tax returns they prepare are incorrect and/or fraudulent. The burden on taxpayers can include receiving an incorrect refund amount or even owing the IRS penalties and interest. As such, the IRS has developed processes and procedures through which taxpayers[1] can file a complaint with the IRS.

To file a complaint, taxpayers complete and mail Form 14157, *Complaint: Tax Return Preparer*,[2] to the IRS Complaint Referrals Office (CRO), which is located in the IRS RPO. The

---

[1] Tax return preparers may also file a complaint against another return preparer. These complaints are not distinguished and are included as taxpayer complaints for the purposes of this report.
[2] See Appendix IV for a copy of Form 14157.

CRO is responsible for collecting the complaints, and cataloguing and building preliminary case files for review, including consolidating the processing of Form 14157 complaints to enable the IRS to better identify problematic tax return preparers and trends in tax return preparer compliance.

The Form 14157 is available on the IRS's public website, IRS.gov; at Taxpayer Assistance Centers[3] located throughout the Nation; and by calling the IRS toll-free telephone line. The CRO has established four phases to process complaints: receipt and control, scoring and prioritization, treatment determination, and manager review. Processing begins when the CRO clerk receives a Form 14157.[4] Once received, the clerk enters information from the Form 14157 into a spreadsheet (the IRS refers to this as the Master Inventory spreadsheet). The clerk then scans and saves an electronic copy of the Form 14157. Once this is completed, a CRO manager assigns the complaint to a case processor. Case processors are responsible for assigning a complaint category and allegation type to each complaint based on the allegation information detailed in the Form 14157 and any supporting evidence. Figure 2 shows the complaint categories and allegation types.

---

[3] An IRS office with employees who answer questions, provide assistance, and resolve account-related issues for taxpayers face to face.
[4] This report describes processes in place on September 11, 2013.

Figure 2: Complaint Categories and Allegation Types

Complaint Category	Allegation Type
E-File Issues	Tax return preparer who allows others to use his or her Electronic Filing Identification Number,[5] fails to file taxpayers' tax returns, or commits other e-file violations.
Tax Return Preparer Misconduct	Tax return preparer who misrepresents his or her credentials or qualifications, commits identity theft, or discloses taxpayers' Personally Identifiable Information.
RPO Program Noncompliance	Tax return preparer who has no Preparer Tax Identification Number (PTIN)[6] or commits PTIN misuse; fails to provide a copy of a return or original records to the taxpayer; commits Circular 230 violations,[7] commits Internal Revenue Code violations that are subject to penalties; or fails to explain refund anticipation loans.
Tax Preparation Noncompliance	Tax return preparer who claims false exemptions or dependents for taxpayers or claims false expenses, deductions, or credits.
Theft of Refund	Tax return preparer who negotiates a taxpayer's refund check, files a tax return that does not match the client's copy, or diverts a taxpayer's refund into an unknown bank account.

Source: *RPO Violation and Treatment Matrix.*

Case processors are also responsible for scoring and prioritizing the complaints based on information in the Form 14157, as well as the number of tax returns filed by the tax return preparer and any history of prior complaints. Case processors use the *Prioritization Matrix* to assign the complaint a score and priority. This matrix is used by the case processors to assign a score based on the seriousness, risk, and severity associated with the complaint. The risk is based on the number of returns filed by the tax return preparer and the percentage of their e-filed returns that the IRS rejected. The complaint is assigned one of the following three scores:[8]

- **Criminal/Egregious Allegations (Score of 5)** – assigned to referrals that include refund theft, identity theft, disclosure of a taxpayer's Personally Identifiable Information, and tax return preparer threats or bribes.

- **Serious Programmatic and Tax Preparation Allegations (Score of 3)** – assigned to referrals that include failure to explain refund anticipation loans, tax return preparer

---

[5] An identification number the IRS assigns to accepted applicants for participation in the IRS e-file Program.

[6] An identification number issued by the IRS that paid tax return preparers must use on tax returns they prepare.

[7] 31 U.S.C. § 330 authorizes the Secretary of the Treasury to regulate the practice of representatives before the Department of the Treasury. The Department of the Treasury issued Regulations Governing Practice before the IRS in Treasury Circular No. 230.

[8] The IRS does not use Score 2 or 4.

provided incorrect filing status of taxpayer, tax return preparer lied about self or credentials, or other misrepresentation.

- **<u>Minor Allegations (Score of 1)</u>** – assigned to referrals that include contested tax return preparation fees, e-file issues, no PTIN, or PTIN misuse.

After case processors score and prioritize the complaints, a CRO manager assigns the complaint to a case specialist who performs research to determine which IRS business function should work the complaint. Some complaints can be addressed by the RPO's Compliance Office[9] or the CRO. The more serious complaints are referred to a business function such as Criminal Investigation. Case specialists consider the complaint categories detailed in Figure 2 and use the *Violation and Treatment Matrix* when deciding to which business function a complaint should be referred.

Once a case specialist makes a referral determination, he or she completes a closing checksheet for manager review and approval. The CRO manager reviews and approves the closing checksheet and forwards it along with the complaint package containing the Form 14157 to the CRO clerk. The CRO clerk then forwards the referral package to the business function based on criteria that each function established.[10] Figure 3 provides the business functions that receive the most complaint referrals and the actions they can take to address the complaints.

---

[9] The RPO Compliance Office is responsible for identifying noncompliant tax return preparers, including the planning and directing of enforcement activities conducted by other IRS functions.
[10] See Appendix V for a hypothetical example of a complaint processed by the CRO.

Figure 3: Enforcement Actions That Business
Functions Can Take to Address Complaints

IRS Business Function	Enforcement Action(s) That Can Be Taken
Criminal Investigation	Initiate investigations of tax fraud related to tax return preparers such as refund or identity theft and recommend cases for prosecution to U.S. Attorney's Offices nationwide and the U.S. Department of Justice.
Office of Professional Responsibility	Analyze, investigate, and interpret alleged practitioner misconduct in violation of Circular 230 and propose disciplinary action; negotiate an appropriate level of discipline with a practitioner or initiate an administrative proceeding to censure (a public reprimand); suspend (one to 59 months) or disbar (five years) the practitioner; or propose a monetary penalty against any practitioner who engages in conduct subject to sanction.
RPO – Compliance Office and CRO	Identify noncompliant tax return preparers, and plan and direct enforcement activities to be conducted across the IRS. For example, the Compliance Office or the CRO can send a warning or educational letter when warranted.
Small Business/ Self-Employed Division Examination Function and Lead Development Centers	Assess penalties and can refer cases to the U.S. Department of Justice for injunction for activities related to the promotion of abusive tax shelters,[11] or aiding or abetting understatement of tax liabilities.[12]

Source: Treasury Inspector General for Tax Administration (TIGTA) analysis of business function responsibilities.

Taxpayers follow an alternate process if they believe a return preparer filed or altered their tax return without consent

Taxpayers who believe a tax return preparer filed or altered their tax return without consent can request that the IRS adjust their tax accounts. These taxpayers must complete Form 14157-A, *Tax Return Preparer Fraud or Misconduct Affidavit.* Taxpayers mail the Form 14157-A, supporting documentation, and a Form 14157 to the IRS's Wage and Investment Division Accounts Management function in Memphis, Tennessee. Representatives in the Accounts Management function scan the forms and supporting documentation into the Correspondence Imaging System (CIS),[13] adjust tax accounts when appropriate, and determine if the complaint relates to tax return preparer misconduct. Examples of complaints that warrant a tax adjustment include substantiated complaints involving math errors by the tax return preparer and complaints

---

[11] 26 U.S.C. § 6700.
[12] 26 U.S.C. § 6701.
[13] A system for scanning all Accounts Management function adjustments receipts into digital images. An electronic workflow delivers the cases to customer service representatives who work the cases from those paperless images.

that the tax return preparer altered the tax return after the taxpayer signed it. The Accounts Management function received 4,024 Forms 14157-A in Fiscal Year[14] 2013 for which a taxpayer requested a tax adjustment.

A prior TIGTA review identified concerns with IRS processing of taxpayer complaints against tax return preparers

In a prior review,[15] we reported that taxpayers who wanted to file a complaint against a paid tax return preparer did not have adequate reporting guidelines and were asked to provide information to the IRS that they may not have known, such as the tax return preparer's designation, *i.e.*, unenrolled agent or practitioner,[16] and whether the complaint involved fraud or a violation of the tax code. In addition, the IRS's Form 3949 A, *Information Referral*, which was previously used by taxpayers to file complaints, was too generic and did not provide adequate instructions.

We also reported that the process for handling taxpayer complaints against tax return preparers did not identify potential problem tax return preparers so that the IRS could determine the extent of the problem or how the problem should be addressed. Complaints were not controlled and tracked. For example, the IRS could not determine the volume of complaints or the number of complaints in open or closed status. Moreover, there was no central point of control for the complaints, thus complaints were reviewed multiple times and mailed to multiple offices before most were ultimately destroyed.

TIGTA recommended that the IRS: 1) clarify guidance to taxpayers on IRS.gov regarding the tax return preparer complaint process and 2) develop a form, both web-based and paper, specifically for tax return preparer complaints. This form should be routed to the correct function based on the type of tax return preparer and include information necessary for the IRS to evaluate the legitimacy of the complaint. We also recommended that once a form is developed to capture sufficient information about the complaint, a database(s) or tracking system should be developed to efficiently control the complaints. The IRS agreed to update guidance on IRS.gov and create a cross-functional team to develop recommended action items to identify opportunities for improvement that may include changes to forms and creation of an automated tracking system.

This review was performed at the CROs in Atlanta, Georgia, and Chesterfield, Missouri, and the Accounts Management function in Memphis, Tennessee, during the period July 2013 through April 2014. We also obtained and reviewed information from the RPO in Crystal City, Virginia,

---

[14] Any yearly accounting period, regardless of its relationship to a calendar year. The Federal Government's fiscal year begins on October 1 and ends on September 30.
[15] TIGTA, Ref. No. 2009-40-032, *The Process Taxpayers Must Use to Report Complaints Against Tax Return Preparers Is Ineffective and Causes Unnecessary Taxpayer Burden* (Feb. 2009).
[16] The IRS refers to tax return preparers who are attorneys, certified public accountants, and enrolled agents as practitioners.

during this same time frame. We conducted this performance audit in accordance with generally accepted government auditing standards. Those standards require that we plan and perform the audit to obtain sufficient, appropriate evidence to provide a reasonable basis for our findings and conclusions based on our audit objective. We believe that the evidence obtained provides a reasonable basis for our findings and conclusions based on our audit objective. Detailed information on our audit objective, scope, and methodology is presented in Appendix I. Major contributors to the report are listed in Appendix II.

Results of Review

Complaints Against Tax Return Preparers Are Not Timely Processed

Our review of the 8,354 complaints received in the CRO in CYs 2012 and 2013, as of September 11, 2013, identified 6,926 (83 percent) complaints for which no work to process the complaint was initiated or the complaint was still being processed. Specifically, we found:

- 3,953 (47 percent) complaints for which no work had been initiated to process the complaint. Specifically, a case processor had not started reviewing these complaints to determine if sufficient information was available to process the complaint.

- 2,973 (36 percent) complaints were determined to be processable and were either in the process of being scored and prioritized, waiting for manager assignment to a case specialist, being worked by a case specialist, or referred to a business function. CRO recordkeeping was not adequate to identify the number of complaints in each of these statuses.

- 1,408 (17 percent) complaints were determined to be unprocessable by the CRO due to a lack of sufficient information or because the complaint did not allege tax return preparer misconduct.

- 20 (less than 1 percent) complaints were marked as duplicate complaints in the Master Inventory spreadsheet.

For the 3,953 complaints for which no work was initiated, Figure 4 shows the number and time frame these complaints had been in case processors' inventory as of September 11, 2013.

Figure 4: Time Frame of Complaints With No Work Initiated

Business Days Complaints Were in Inventory With No Work Initiated	Number of Complaints	Percentage
1 to 44 Days	1,595	40%
45 to 59 Days	438	11%
60 to 119 Days	1,896	48%
120 Days or Greater	24	1%
Total	3,953	

Source: CRO CY 2013 Master Inventory spreadsheet.

The lack of timely complaint processing is attributable to a number of reasons that include:

- A higher number of complaints received in CY 2013, as of September 11, 2013, when compared to CY 2012. For example, as of September 11, 2013, the IRS had received 2,069 (33 percent) more complaints than in the same period in CY 2012.

- CRO staff changes. In July 2013, the manager, clerk, and a case specialist left the CRO. The clerk's departure required case processors to perform the clerk's duties, causing case processors to fall behind in scoring and prioritizing complaints. The CRO added four employees in late CY 2013 but needed time to train the staff to process the complaints.

- New procedures were implemented for case processors and case specialists. CRO management updated procedures as complaint processing issues were identified. These revisions created a learning curve for case processors and case specialists that contributed to the untimely complaint processing. For example, the scoring and prioritization process, the *Prioritization Matrix*, and the *Violation and Treatment Matrix* were implemented in February 2013. Management believed that streamlining procedures and tools would reduce the backlog. However, the change in procedures and tools occurred shortly before the time frame that most complaints against tax return preparers are received.

In addition, CRO guidelines suggest case processors spend 10 to 15 minutes to score and prioritize a complaint, and case specialists have 30 to 60 minutes to complete their research, make a treatment determination, and complete the closing checksheet. A business case analysis was not performed for use as a basis when developing these complaint processing time frames. IRS procedures require managers to set performance goals and measure the effectiveness of their programs, including the timeliness of completing work. Expectations must be specific, measurable, realistic, and attainable. Management officials plan to establish time frame goals after they reduce the backlog of complaints.

*********************************3***
****

3
3*.
CRO management has not established a time frame for how long the clerk has to record a complaint in the Master Inventory spreadsheet after IRS receipt. ********3*********
3
3**********************************. In
addition, a process was not established to periodically reconcile the number of complaints received to the number recorded in the Master Inventory spreadsheet. The lack of reconciliation between the number of complaints received to the number controlled in the Master Inventory spreadsheet along with the inadequate segregation of receipt and control duties could create an

environment in which complaints can be lost or destroyed by an employee without detection. Currently, the clerk performs both the receipt and control duties.

Recommendations

The Deputy Commissioner for Services and Enforcement should:

Recommendation 1: Establish complaint processing time frame goals that are based on a business case analysis. Once these time frame goals are developed, establish procedures to ensure that the complaints are timely processed.

> ***Management's Response:*** IRS management agreed with this recommendation. IRS management stated they are in the process of developing goals that will measure specific components of complaint processing, including timeliness. The IRS stated that developing the goals will be an iterative process over time.

Recommendation 2: Ensure that adequate separation of duties exists in receipt and recording of complaints into inventory records. In addition, establish a process to periodically reconcile the number of complaints received to the number recorded in the Master Inventory spreadsheet to ensure that all complaints are controlled.

> ***Management's Response:*** IRS management agreed with this recommendation. IRS management stated they have already implemented the separation of duties related to receipt and recording of complaints into inventory records. The IRS will also periodically reconcile the number of complaints received to the number recorded in the Return Preparer database,[17] recognizing that there is no direct correlation between pieces of mail and the number of complaints received.

Processes Do Not Ensure That Complaints Are Accurately and Consistently Processed

Our review of a statistically valid sample[18] of 73 of 8,354 complaints received in CYs 2012 and 2013, as of September 11, 2013, found that an adequate process had not been established to ensure that complaints are accurately and consistently processed. For example, of the 73 complaints we reviewed, 31 had not been fully processed by case processors and 17 could not

---

[17] The Return Preparer database includes preparer demographic information and aggregate data, by preparer, for the volume of returns, the volume of returns by filing method (paper or e-file), returns with refunds, and returns with balances due. The primary users of the database are the RPO, Return Preparer Coordinators, and Criminal Investigation.

[18] We selected a statistical sample of 73 complaints from a population of 8,354 complaints scanned into the CRO's fileserver as Portable Document Format files for CY 2013 using a 95 percent confidence level, a ± 5 percent precision rate, and a 5 percent error rate.

be processed due to a lack of sufficient information or because the complaint did not allege tax return preparer misconduct.

The remaining 25 complaints were worked and completed. However, we were unable to determine for these 25 complaints if they were properly ranked, scored, and/or prioritized because each case processor applied risk ranking elements differently. For example, **3****
*************************************3**
****************.[19] ************************3************************************

Whereas another case processor measured risk using only the return preparer's e file rejection rate.

Case processors must assign a priority to the complaints by evaluating the risk associated with the complaint and assigning one of four priority levels: urgent, high, priority, or low. Correctly assigning a priority level for the risk is important because the score contributes to the overall priority ranking which determines when the complaint is worked. Inconsistency in measuring risk can result in the IRS using limited resources investigating tax return preparers who do not pose a high level of risk to tax administration. Figure 5 provides the Risk Ranking Chart that was used by case processors.

Figure 5: Risk Ranking Chart

High Volume Tax Return Preparer With Problematic E-File Submissions (Score of 3)	Medium Volume Tax Return Preparer With Questionable E-File Submissions (Score of 2)	Low Volume Tax Return Preparer With Acceptable E-File Submissions (Score of 1)
> 500 returns in prior year	100 to 500 returns in prior year	< 100 returns in prior year
> 50 percent e-file rejection rate	10 to 50 percent e-file rejection rate	< 10 percent e-file rejection rate

Source: IRS CRO.

However, despite the importance of risk ranking, the CRO had not developed a sufficient risk ranking guide for case processors. For example, the Risk Ranking Chart used by case processors did not take into account the myriad of different scenarios that are often associated with complaints being reviewed. For example, the Risk Ranking Chart did not address a scenario in which the return volumes and e-file rejections could fall in more than one category, such as 300 e-filed returns with an e-file rejection rate of 3 percent. In this scenario, the case processor must make a determination whether to use the e-file rejection rate of less than 10 percent, which would result in a low risk ranking score, or rank the complaint based on the volume of 300 e-filed returns, which would result in a medium risk ranking score.

---

[19] The e-file rejection rate is determined by dividing the number of tax returns rejected by the number of e-filed tax returns.

When we brought this issue to management's attention, they indicated that revisions to the Risk Ranking Chart had not been made because they were in the process of reviewing all CRO processes as part of their development of a new Operating Procedures Desk Guide. It should be noted that concerns regarding the ambiguity of the Risk Ranking Chart were also raised during a training session held in February 2014 in which the Risk Ranking Chart was discussed. Case processors and managers attending the session could not agree on how to assign risk rankings to complaint scenarios being reviewed as part of the training session. They agreed the current Risk Ranking Chart is confusing. In March 2014, the CRO published new risk ranking procedures for use by its employees. However, we did not evaluate these new procedures because they were implemented subsequent to the completion of our audit testing.

Processes have not been established to effectively track complaint referrals to business functions

The CRO has not established procedures to track complaints that it refers to IRS business functions to ensure that the complaints are received for evaluation nor does the CRO track how the referred complaints are ultimately resolved. For example, resolution and closure actions taken by the business functions were not recorded in the Master Inventory spreadsheet.

Our review of a statistically valid sample[20] of 67 complaints from the population of 741 that were referred to business functions in CY 2013, as of September 11, 2013, found that the business functions had no record of receiving 19 (28 percent) complaints. In addition, for 14 complaints closed with no action, five[21] did not meet the functions' criteria for referring the complaint, and**1*********************. Figure 6 provides the resolution of the 67 complaints we evaluated.

---

[20] We selected a statistical sample of 67 complaints from a population of 741 complaints referred to the three business functions that received the most referrals using a 95 percent confidence level, a ± 5 percent precision rate, and a 5 percent error rate.

[21] **1***.

Figure 6: Resolution of Complaints Referred to IRS Business Functions

Resolution	Number of Complaints	Percentage[22]
Open – ongoing investigation	19	28%
Business function had no record of receiving complaint – For five, we could not identify to which function the complaint was referred.	19	28%
Referred for enforcement action – Seven were referred to the Department of Justice (four for injunction and three for criminal prosecution). Six were referred to the Small Business/Self-Employed Division for penalty assessment. Two were referred to the Lead Development Center for penalty assessment.	15	22%
Closed – No action was taken for eight because the allegation could not be substantiated, for five because the complaint did not meet the business functions' referral criteria, and for one because the complaint lacked sufficient information to conduct an investigation.	14	21%

Source: TIGTA analysis of 67 sampled complaints that the CRO referred to business functions in CY 2013.

The CRO is responsible for reviewing complaints to identify the correct business function that will work the complaint. In order to identify which function will work the complaints, the CRO compares the complaint information against referral criteria established by the functions. However, the lack of a process to track complaint resolutions by the business functions prevented the CRO from identifying errors such as the five complaints in our sample that did not meet the functions' referral criteria. In addition, without complaint resolution tracking, the CRO cannot ensure that the business functions are receiving the complaints for evaluation.

Current procedures instruct case specialists to send all complaints associated with a project case directly to the revenue agent working the case. This procedure sometimes results in the complaint referral bypassing the business functions' designated point of contact, which is responsible for tracking the incoming complaints. For example, Criminal Investigation's point of contact could not account for four complaints in our sample that were routed directly to agents. If not located, these complaints cannot be used to initiate and build a case against a return preparer. ******************1*************************************** ******************************1*** ******************************1*** *******************1***************.

---

[22] Percentages do not total 100 due to rounding.

Processes for contacting taxpayers to obtain missing complaint information have not been established

Case processors determined that 1,408 (32 percent) of the 4,401 complaints that they reviewed in CY 2013, through September 11, 2013, were unable to be processed as a result of missing information in the Form 14157 or because the complaint did not allege tax return preparer misconduct. However, the case processors did not attempt to obtain the missing information because they were not required to contact the taxpayer in an effort to obtain the needed information. We found 744 (53 percent) of the 1,408 complaints had a taxpayer address or telephone number that the case processors could have used in an effort to contact the taxpayer.

Management had not established procedures for case processors to contact taxpayers in an attempt to obtain missing complaint information. Without processes to obtain the missing information, the IRS's ability to identify problem return preparers is diminished and can affect the IRS's enforcement actions. Management stated that they did not have the resources to contact taxpayers to obtain missing information and there was no way to know that contacting the complainant would yield the necessary information to allow processing.

Duplicate scanning of Form 14157 results in inefficient use of resources

The CRO has not obtained access to the CIS, which contains electronic images of Forms 14157 and supporting documentation that may have been received from taxpayers. The Forms 14157 scanned into the CIS are those that are received in the IRS's Accounts Management function when a taxpayer submits a Form 14157-A. Because CRO employees do not have access to the CIS, customer service representatives in the Accounts Management function have to mail duplicate copies of Forms 14157 and any supporting documentation to the CRO even though this information was scanned into the CIS. The Accounts Management function mailed 312 Forms 14157 including supporting documentation to the CRO during CY 2013.

The procedure requiring customer service representatives to mail paper Forms 14157 to the CRO results in the inefficient use of resources in both functions. Customer service representatives waste time mailing the forms, and the CRO clerk wastes time rescanning the forms into the office's fileserver. CRO management indicated that they did not obtain access to the CIS for their employees because they had implemented new procedures and believed gaining access to another system was too much to take on.

Recommendations

The Deputy Commissioner for Services and Enforcement should:

Recommendation 3: Ensure that criteria for referring complaints to other IRS business functions are appropriately applied.

Management's Response: IRS management agreed with this recommendation. IRS management stated they now include the IRS business function's point of contact on all referrals so the contact may notify the RPO if the referral criteria were not met. Also, the IRS plans to address proper application of referral criteria during any refresher training, quality reviews, and managerial reviews of complaint processing.

Recommendation 4: Develop a process that accurately tracks complaints that the CRO refers to IRS business functions to ensure that the complaints are received for evaluation. In addition, inventory records should include information as to whether and how the referral was ultimately resolved by the business functions.

Management's Response: IRS management partially agreed with this recommendation. IRS management agreed it is important to ensure that all complaints are received by the IRS business function to which they were referred and have already established an assurance process. IRS management stated that they now send all referrals via e-mail requesting confirmation that the e-mail was read. Receipt messages are reconciled periodically with sent items. Unreconciled items are investigated.

IRS management agreed that it is important to ensure that referred complaints meet the business functions referral criteria and the inventory records include complaint resolution information. However, rather than tracking the ultimate resolution of each referred complaint, IRS management will instead use the quarterly stakeholder referral meetings as an opportunity to regularly discuss whether referrals were productive and to reassess the continued viability of referral criteria. This will achieve the same result with far fewer of the limited resources than would be required to track every referral.

Office of Audit Comment: TIGTA continues to believe IRS management should track how the business functions resolve referred complaints. Resolution information will provide more detailed information and allow the CRO to evaluate the accuracy of the referral criteria in place.

Recommendation 5: Ensure that the CRO establishes procedures for case processors to contact taxpayers for missing information in order to work as many complaints as possible.

Management's Response: IRS management disagreed with this recommendation. IRS management stated that they are focused on reducing the current backlog of complaints and maintaining currency of complaint processing. Once the IRS is able to sustain currency and should the IRS have sufficient resources, it will consider designing a pilot test for contacting complainants who submit incomplete information as well as an address or telephone number to ascertain the viability and cost-effectiveness of such contacts. At this time, however, the IRS does not have the resources to contact complainants or conduct such a pilot.

Office of Audit Comment: TIGTA continues to believe that taxpayers should be contacted for missing information on submitted complaints. Working more complaints will provide the CRO with information to identify problem return preparers. While we understand the resource limitations IRS management noted in its response, we believe, at a minimum, IRS management should conduct a pilot test for contacting complainants who submit incomplete information as soon as possible.

Recommendation 6: Ensure that access to the CIS is provided to CRO employees to allow them to download electronic copies of Forms 14157 and related documents.

Management's Response: IRS management agreed with this recommendation. IRS management stated they have already obtained CIS access for their employees so they may download electronic copies of Forms 14157 and related documents.

Some Recommendations Reported in a Prior Treasury Inspector General for Tax Administration Report Have Been Addressed

The IRS has completed corrective actions that partially address the two recommendations included in our prior report. Guidance was developed and posted on IRS.gov, and in June 2009, the IRS initiated the Return Preparer Review to strengthen partnerships with tax practitioners. As a result of this internal review, the IRS created the RPO in October 2010 to oversee and support tax professionals. Figure 7 provides the corrective actions the IRS has taken in response to our prior audit.

Figure 7: Corrective Actions Implemented in Response to the Prior TIGTA Audit

Recommendation	Corrective Actions
Clarify guidance on IRS.gov when the taxpayer searches for "preparer complaint" so that taxpayers can understand the differences in the types of tax return preparers, the jurisdiction the IRS has over enrolled and unenrolled tax return preparers, and to which function taxpayer complaints against tax return preparers should be sent.	• When a taxpayer searches on IRS.gov for "complaint" or "preparer complaint," the taxpayer is directed to a webpage that indicates complaints may be filed on Form 14157 and mailed to the RPO in Atlanta, Georgia. • The instructions for Form 14157 properly define the different types of tax return preparers.
Develop a form, both web-based and paper, specifically for tax return preparer complaints that can be routed to the correct function based on the type of tax return preparer and includes the items necessary for the IRS to appropriately evaluate the complaint. Once a form is developed to ensure that sufficient information is captured about the complaint, a database or tracking system should be developed to efficiently control the complaints.	• Form 14157 was developed to capture complaints against tax return preparers and includes items necessary for the IRS to evaluate the complaint. The IRS accepts complaints against tax return preparers via paper Forms 14157. Processes for submitting complaints electronically have not been established due to a perceived lack of resources and funding. • The CRO was delegated responsibility for routing complaints to the correct function based on the type of complaint.

Source: TIGTA auditors' analysis of actions taken in response to a previous audit report.

However, the IRS has not effectively addressed the part of our second recommendation to develop a database(s) or tracking system to efficiently record and track complaints. In CY 2013, the CRO began coordinating with the Small Business/Self-Employed Division to develop a complaint module within the Return Preparer database. Although a complaint module was developed, it does not provide the ability to efficiently and effectively track complaints and analyze trends in return preparer conduct. For example, the complaint module does not provide the business function's resolution of the complaints.

Moreover, the complaint module does not provide the capability to efficiently produce management information reports detailing key measures such as complaint receipts, closures, and status. To obtain this much needed management information, the CRO Director exports the data from the database to an Excel spreadsheet on a monthly basis. The data export includes thousands of rows, a large number of columns, and many formulas that make analysis of the data cumbersome. In addition, management officials noted that the size of the spreadsheet and large amount of data have caused the spreadsheet to crash, *i.e.*, stop functioning, which then requires the CRO Director to have to export the data again.

Data loaded into the complaint module are incomplete

In CY 2014, data from CY 2013 were transferred from the CRO Master Inventory spreadsheet to the new complaint module added to the Return Preparer database. However, the complaint data from CY 2012 were not transferred because it is formatted differently than the CY 2013 data. The CRO determined it would be too time consuming to reformat the CY 2012 data to upload it to the Return Preparer database complaint module in advance of the 2014 Filing Season.[23] The CRO has requested upload of the CY 2012 data during CY 2014 but resources have yet to be made available to complete the reformatting and uploading of the data. Not having the CY 2012 data in the new complaint module requires CRO employees to review the CY 2012 data in the Master Inventory spreadsheet to identify any prior complaints about tax return preparers. Not including the CY 2012 complaint data in the new complaint module diminishes the IRS's ability to identify trends in return preparer conduct.

Recommendations

The Deputy Commissioner for Services and Enforcement should:

Recommendation 7: Ensure that the complaint module in the Return Preparer database is updated to include all data collected on complaints, including the CY 2012 data.

> **Management's Response:** IRS management agreed with this recommendation and stated the CY 2012 complaint data have been uploaded to the Return Preparer database.

Recommendation 8: Develop the capability to produce management information reports from the complaint module in the Return Preparer database.

> **Management's Response:** IRS management agreed with this recommendation. IRS management stated the administrators of the Return Preparer database are currently updating the functionality of the database so it may be used to create management reports.

---

[23] The period from January through mid-April when most individual income tax returns are filed.

Appendix I

Detailed Objective, Scope, and Methodology

Our overall objective was to determine whether the tax return preparer complaint process is effective. We determined if sufficient controls are in place for the IRS to manage and track the complaints, determine the validity of the complaints, and use the data to take enforcement actions. To accomplish our objective, we:

I.   Evaluated the sufficiency of the IRS's procedures and guidelines for processing complaints against tax return preparers (follow-up from prior audit).[1]

II. Determined if there are sufficient controls in place to work, track, and manage the complaints, and determined the validity of the complaints (follow-up from prior audit).

   A. Evaluated the sufficiency of the complaint referrals process from receipt to closure. We selected a statistical sample of 73 complaints from a population of 8,354 complaints scanned into the CRO's fileserver as Portable Document Format files for CY 2013. We used a 95 percent confidence level, a ± 5 percent precision rate, and a 5 percent error rate. We traced the complaints to the Master Inventory spreadsheet to determine completeness and accuracy of data entered in the spreadsheet. We ran a query against the Return Transaction File Preparer Taxpayer Identification Number File to verify the information in the spreadsheet is accurate and matches the data in the Taxpayer Identification Number file.[2] We did not analyze all 8,354 complaints because of staff and time limitations.

   B. Determined if complaint referrals were received by business functions and whether the referrals provided sufficient and relevant information for the functions to work the referrals. We selected a statistical sample of 67 complaints from a population of 741 complaints referred to the three business functions that received the most referrals. We used a 95 percent confidence level, a ± 5 percent precision rate, and a 5 percent error rate. We did not analyze all 741 referrals because of staff and time limitations.

III. Evaluated the controls for ensuring that actions are taken on complaints when warranted.

---

[1] TIGTA, Ref. No. 2009-40-032, *The Process Taxpayers Must Use to Report Complaints Against Tax Return Preparers Is Ineffective and Causes Unnecessary Taxpayer Burden* (Feb. 2009).

[2] Preparer Tax Identification Number File data are extracted from an IRS file known as the PTIN Cross-Reference database. This database is basically a cross-reference of Social Security Numbers and PTINs.

Internal controls methodology

Internal controls relate to management's plans, methods, and procedures used to meet their mission, goals, and objectives. Internal controls include the processes and procedures for planning, organizing, directing, and controlling program operations. They include the systems for measuring, reporting, and monitoring program performance. We determined that the following internal controls were relevant to our audit objective: the IRS's policies, procedures, and practices for processing Forms 14157. We evaluated these controls by interviewing management and employees, examining applicable guidance documents, and reviewing Forms 14157 and related information.

Appendix II

Major Contributors to This Report

Russell P. Martin, Acting Assistant Inspector General for Audit (Returns Processing and
Account Services)
William A. Gray, Director
Paula W. Johnson, Audit Manager
Jean Bell, Lead Auditor
Van Warmke, Senior Auditor
Jerome Antoine, Auditor
Blanche Lavender, Information Technology Specialist

Appendix III

Report Distribution List

Commissioner C
Office of the Commissioner – Attn: Chief of Staff C
Deputy Commissioner for Operations Support OS
Chief Counsel CC
Chief, Criminal Investigation SE:CI
Commissioner, Small Business/Self-Employed Division SE:S
Commissioner, Wage and Investment Division SE:W
National Taxpayer Advocate TA
Director, Office of Professional Responsibility SE:OPR
Director, Return Preparer Office SE:RPO
Director, Customer Account Services, Wage and Investment Division SE:W:CAS
Director, Customer Assistance, Relationships, and Education, Wage and Investment Division SE:W:CAR
Director, Examination, Small Business/Self-Employed Division SE:S:E
Director, Strategy and Finance, Wage and Investment Division SE:W:S
Senior Operations Advisor, Wage and Investment Division SE:W:S
Director, Accounts Management, Wage and Investment Division SE:W:CAS:AM
Director, Field Assistance, Wage and Investment Division SE:W:CAR:FA
Director, Office of Legislative Affairs CL:LA
Director, Office of Program Evaluation and Risk Analysis RAS:O
Office of Internal Control OS:CFO:CPIC:IC
Audit Liaison: Chief, Program Evaluation and Improvement, Wage and Investment Division SE:W:S:PEI

Appendix IV

Form 14157, Complaint: Tax Return Preparer

Form **14157** (Rev. August 2013)	Department of the Treasury - Internal Revenue Service **Complaint: Tax Return Preparer**	OMB Number 1545-2168

Use this form to file a complaint with the IRS against a tax return preparer or tax preparation business.

CAUTION: READ THE INSTRUCTIONS BEFORE COMPLETING THIS FORM. There may be other more appropriate forms specific to your complaint. (For example, if you believe you are a victim of identity theft, please complete Form 14039, Identity Theft Affidavit).

Section A - Return Preparer Information *(complete all known information)*

1. Preparer's professional status *(check all that apply)*

[ ] Attorney　　　　　　　　　　　　　　　[ ] Certified Public Accountant

[ ] Enrolled Agent　　　　　　　　　　　　[ ] Other/Unknown

2. Preparer's name and address	3. Preparer's business name and address *(if different)*
4. Preparer's telephone number(s) *(include area code)*	5. Preparer's email address
6. Preparer's website	7. Preparer Electronic Filing Identification Number (EFIN)
8. Preparer Tax Identification Number (PTIN)	9. Employer Identification Number (EIN)

Section B - Complaint Information

10. Tax year(s) impacted

11a. Review the complaints below and check all that apply

[ ] Theft of Refund *(Diverted refund to unknown account; return filed does not match taxpayer's copy)*

[ ] E-File *(e-filed returns using pay stub; e-filed returns using non-commercial software or Free File; e-filed returns without properly securing taxpayer's signature)*

[ ] Preparer Misconduct *(Failure to provide copy of return; failure to return records; failure to sign returns; misrepresentation of credentials; agreed to file return but did not; failure to remit payment for taxes due; filed return without authorization or consent; failure to explain Refund Anticipation Loans (RALs))*

[ ] PTIN Issues *(Failure to include Preparer Tax Identification Number (PTIN) on tax return; improperly using a PTIN belonging to another individual)*

[ ] False Items/Documents *(False expenses, deductions, or credits; false exemptions or dependents; false or altered documents; false or overstated Form W-2 or 1099; incorrect filing status)*

[ ] Employment Taxes *(Failure to file or remit Employment Tax payment)*

[ ] Other *(explain below)*

Attach a copy of any documents you received from the tax return preparer (e.g. **tax returns**, advertisements, business cards, Form 8879, IRS e-file Signature Authorization, Form 8888, Allocation of Refund (including savings bond purchases), and Refund Transfer Agreement).

Catalog Number 55242M　　　　　　　www.irs.gov　　　　　　Form **14157** (Rev. 8-2013)

11b. Provide facts and other information related to the complaint *(attach additional sheets if necessary).*

Section C - Taxpayer's Information

(We never share this information with the person or business you are reporting)
This information is not required to process your complaint but is helpful if we need to contact you for additional information.

12. Name *(Last, First, MI)*

13. Mailing address *(street, city, state, ZIP code)*

14. Telephone number(s) *(include area code)*

15. Email address

16. Taxpayer's signature

17. Date of complaint

Section D - Your Information *(do not complete if you are the taxpayer)*

(We never share this information with the person or business you are reporting)
This information is not required to process your complaint but is helpful if we need to contact you for additional information.

18. Name *(Last, First, MI)*

19. Date of complaint

20. Mailing address *(street, city, state, ZIP code)*

21. Telephone number(s) *(include area code)*

22. Email address

23. Your relationship to Preparer

☐ Client

☐ IRS employee

☐ Return preparer working for a different firm*

☐ Other *(specify)* _____

☐ Return preparer working for the same firm*

* Taxpayers' information and any information relating to another professional are confidential. Please obtain your client's consent before sharing any protected tax information, even with the IRS.

Send completed form along with all supporting information to:

Attn: Return Preparer Office
401 W. Peachtree Street NW
Mail Stop 421-D
Atlanta, GA 30308

Privacy Act and Paperwork Reduction Act Notice

We ask for the information on this form to carry out the Internal Revenue laws of the United States. We need it to ensure that preparers are complying with these laws and to allow us to figure and collect the right amount of tax.

You are not required to provide the information requested on a form that is subject to the Paperwork Reduction Act unless the form displays a valid OMB control number. Books or records relating to a form or its instructions must be retained as long as their contents may become material in the administration of any Internal Revenue law. Generally, tax returns and return information are confidential, as required by Internal Revenue Code section 6103.

The time require to complete this form will vary depending on individual circumstances. The estimated average time is 15 minutes. The primary purpose of this form is to report potential violations of the Internal Revenue laws by tax return preparers. We are requesting this information under authority of 26 U.S.C. § 7801 and § 7803. Providing this information is voluntary, and failure to provide all or part of the information will not affect you. Providing false or fraudulent information may subject you to penalties. We may disclose this information to the Department of Justice to enforce the tax laws, both civil and criminal, and to cities, states, the District of Columbia, and U.S. commonwealths or possessions to carry out their tax laws. We may also disclose this information to other countries under a tax treaty, to federal and state agencies to enforce federal non-tax criminal laws, and to federal law enforcement and intelligence agencies to combat terrorism.

Catalog Number 55242M

www.irs.gov

Form **14157** (Rev. 8-2013)

Instructions for Form 14157, Complaint: Tax Return Preparer

General Instructions

What's New

The number of check boxes was reduced to avoid confusion. A section was added to obtain information relevant to the impacted taxpayer.

Purpose of Form

Use Form 14157 to file a complaint against a tax return preparer or tax preparation business.

Individuals who are paid to prepare federal tax returns must follow ethical standards and guidelines as established in Treasury Department Circular 230. For more information on requirements for paid tax return preparers, view Circular 230 at www.irs.gov/taxpros.

Where to Send This Form

Send completed form along with all supporting information to:

Attn: Return Preparer Office
401 W. Peachtree Street NW
Mail Stop 421-D
Atlanta, GA 30308

CAUTION: DO NOT USE Form 14157:

- If you suspect your **identity was stolen**. Use Form 14039. Follow "Instructions for Submitting this Form" on Page 2 of Form 14039.

- If a **tax return preparer** filed a return or altered your return **without your consent** and you are seeking a change to your account, complete Form 14157-A, Tax Return Preparer Fraud or Misconduct Affidavit and this form. Submit both forms along with the documents listed in the Form 14157-A instructions to the address shown on that form.

- To report **alleged tax law** violations by an individual, a business, or both. Use Form 3949-A. Submit to the address on the Form 3949-A.

Specific Instructions

Section A - Return Preparer Information

Preparer's Professional Status - Indicate any professional credentials held, or claimed to be held, by the return preparer. An Attorney is an individual in good standing with a state bar association. A Certified Public Accountant is an individual in good standing with a state board of accountancy. An Enrolled Agent status is granted solely by the IRS upon the individual's demonstration of special competence in tax matters, by written examination, and passing suitability requirements. Select Other/Unknown if you are unsure of the preparer's status.

Information about the Tax Return Preparer - Provide as much information as you know about the paid tax return preparer or business.

Preparer's Identification Numbers(s) - If known, provide the tax preparer's Electronic Filing Identification Number (EFIN), Preparer Tax Identification Number (PTIN), and Employer Identification Number (EIN).

Section B - Complaint Information

Tax Year(s)

Indicate the tax year(s) of the tax return for which the tax preparer misconduct occurred. Most individual's tax returns cover a calendar year of 12 months, January 1 through December 31. For example, you may have a tax return that was prepared in 2012, but the tax year is 2011 because the tax return covered calendar year 2011.

Review the complaint allegations and check all that apply. Describe in detail the facts of your complaint in 11b. Attach a copy of any documents you received from the tax return preparer. Also attach additional sheets if necessary.

Theft of Refund

A preparer:
- Embezzled or stole all or a portion of a client's federal tax refund.
- Diverted a refund to an account that was not the client's.
- Provided a copy of the return to the client that had direct deposit information that is not theirs.
- Provided a copy of the return to the client that does not match the return that was filed with the IRS.
- Failed to explain that a cash advance, fast refund, or instant refund was actually a refund anticipation loan borrowed against an income tax refund and the related fees and interest charges.

Catalog Number 55242M   www.irs.gov   Form **14157** (Rev. 8-2013)

E-File

A preparer:
- Filed a return electronically using a last payroll stub or a leave and earnings statement without waiting for the official Form W-2 from the employer. Return preparers are generally prohibited from filing a return prior to receipt of Forms W-2, W-2G, and 1099-R.
- Used non-commercial software to prepare returns that appear self prepared by the taxpayer and is not including his or her name, PTIN, or firm name. Similarly, the preparer used the "Free File" program to prepare and file tax returns for clients. For more information on Free File, visit www.irs.gov/freefile.
- Filed a return electronically without securing taxpayer's signature on Form 8879 (e-File Signature Authorization).

Preparer Misconduct

A preparer:
- Did not provide client with a copy of the return he or she prepared, and refused to provide a copy after a request.
- Did not return some or all of the client's original records.
- Did not sign the federal tax returns that he or she prepared.
- Claimed to be an attorney, certified public accountant, enrolled agent, or registered tax return preparer, but does not actually have the credential claimed or the credential is no longer valid (e.g. expired, suspended or revoked).
- Agreed to file return but did not - The preparer charged for services not performed.
- Did not remit payment for taxes due
- Filed a return or submitted other information for a client without their knowledge, authorization, or consent.
- Failed to explain that a cash advance, fast refund, or instant refund was actually a refund anticipation loan borrowed against an income tax refund and the related fees and interest charges. The return preparer was misleading, or failed to ensure taxpayers understand financial products and related fees.

PTIN Issues

A preparer:
- Improperly used a Preparer Tax Identification Number (PTIN) belonging to another individual.
- Does not have a PTIN or is not including a PTIN on returns prepared.

False Items/Documents

A preparer knowingly:
- Claimed false or fictitious expenses and/or deductions on a tax return.
- Claimed unrelated, non-existent, unknown or additional information on a tax return.
- Made changes to a client's original tax documents or used false or incorrect documents to complete return.
- Claimed false or fictitious income and/or federal withholding on a tax return.
- Claimed an improper filing status on a tax return. The filing status claimed did not accurately reflect the taxpayer's family situation.

Employment Taxes

A preparer:

- Did not remit employment tax funds to the IRS on behalf of a client for Forms 940, 941, 943, 944, or 945.

Other

- If none of the above describes the nature of the complaint, briefly summarize the complaint. Some examples of other tax preparer misconduct or improper tax preparation practices include, but are not limited to, fee dispute and bad behavior such as threats.

Section C - Taxpayer Information

Enter the taxpayer's name, street address, city, state, zip code, telephone number(s), and email address where he/she can be contacted.

Taxpayer's Signature – Sign and date. The taxpayer's signature is necessary if Form 14157 is completed by another individual.

Section D - Your Contact Information

Enter your name, street address, city, state, zip code, telephone number(s), and e-mail address where you can be contacted. This information is not required to process your complaint but is helpful if we need to contact you for additional information.

Your Relationship to Preparer

Enter your relationship to the return preparer.

Taxpayers' information and any information relating to another professional are confidential. Please obtain your client's consent before sharing any protected tax information, even with the IRS.

Appendix V

Complaint Processing Example

The following hypothetical example illustrates the IRS's processing of complaints against tax return preparers.

> *The CRO received a Form 14157, Complaint: Tax Return Preparer, in CY 2013 from Complainant A. Complainant A selected "False Items" on the Form 14157 alleging the tax return preparer put false deductions and credits on the tax return which reduced the tax liability and inflated the refund amount. The tax return preparer e-filed 2,554 tax returns in Processing Year[1] 2012 and the IRS rejected 1,303 of these returns. There is no ongoing investigation of the tax return preparer, but another complainant filed a complaint for a similar allegation against this tax return preparer in CY 2012.*

Case Processor Steps

1. Determine if a case has an ongoing investigation in an IRS function.

   ➤ *Example: No ongoing investigation.*

2. Select the complaint category based on information on the Form 14157.

Complaint Categories				
E-File Issues	Return Preparer Misconduct	RPO Program Noncompliance	Tax Preparation Noncompliance	Theft of Refund

   ➤ *Example: Tax Preparation Noncompliance.*

---

[1] The calendar year in which the tax return or document is processed by the IRS.

3. Determine seriousness ranking.

Seriousness Ranking		
Criminal/Egregious Allegations	**Serious Programmatic and Tax Preparation Allegations**	**Minor Allegations**
Score of 5	Score of 3	Score of 1
a. *Theft of Refund*	j. *Failure to Explain Refund Anticipation Loans*	q. *Contested Return Preparation Fee*
b. *Return Preparer Commits Identity Theft of a Taxpayer, or Discloses Personally Identifiable Information*	k. *Return Preparer Provides Incorrect Filing Status of Taxpayer*	r. *Failure to Provide Copy of Return or Original Records to Taxpayer*
c. *Failure to Remit Employment Tax Payment*	l. *Return Preparer Files Taxpayer Return With Unreported Income/False or Overstated Forms W-2, Wage and Tax Statement, or Forms 1099*	s. *All E-File Issues*
d. *Return Preparer Threatens or Bribes a Taxpayer*	m. *Complaints Against Noncompensated Return Preparers*	t. *No PTIN or Misuse*
e. *Organized Crime/Kickbacks/Narcotics/ Wagering/Gambling*	n. *All Other Circular 230 Violations*	
f. *Return Preparer Acts on Behalf of Taxpayer Without Authorization or Consent Due to False or Altered Documents*	o. *All other Internal Revenue Code Violations*	
g. *False Expenses, Deductions, or Credits*	p. *Preparer Lies About Self or Credentials, or Other Misrepresentation*	
h. *Return Preparer Claims False Exemptions or Dependents for Taxpayer*		
i. *Fraudulent Earned Income Credit (Form 3949A, Information Referral)*		

➤ *Example: Criminal/Egregious Allegation for False Expenses, Deductions, or Credits (Score of 5).*

4. Determine risk ranking.

Risk Ranking		
	Medium Volume Preparer With Questionable E-File Submissions (Score of 2)	Low Volume Preparer With Acceptable E-File Submissions (Score of 1)
> 500 returns in prior year	100 to 500 returns in prior year	< 100 returns in prior year
> 50 percent e-file rejection rate	10 to 50 percent e-file rejection rate	< 10 percent e-file rejection rate

> ➤ *Example: High Volume Preparer With Problematic E-File Submissions (Score of 3).*

5. Determine severity ranking.

Severity Ranking		
Egregious Score of 3	Serious Score of 2	Minor Score of 1
> Three complaints	Two complaints	One complaint

> ➤ *Example: Serious (Score of 2)*

6. Sum seriousness, risk, and severity rankings to determine priority.

Priority Ranking		
High Priority	Priority	Low Priority
Total score from 9 to 11	Total score from 6 to 8	Total score from 3 to 5

> ➤ *Example: High Priority (Score of 10 (5 plus 3 plus 2))*

Case Specialist, Manager, and Clerk Steps

1. Consider the complaint category and allegation type to ensure that the most egregious issue is researched and pursued.

> ➤ *Example: Complaint Category "Tax Return Preparation Noncompliance" with Allegation Type "False Expenses, Deductions, or Credits."*

2. Conduct research on IRS systems to confirm allegation.

    ➢ *Example: The complainant submitted a Form 1040, U.S. Individual Income Tax. The case specialist compares the e-filed Form 1040 transmitted by the return preparer to determine if the allegation of false deductions and credits can be substantiated. The research showed that the Form 1040 e-filed by the preparer has different deductions than the complainant's copy of the Form 1040.*

3. Determine the treatment.

    ➢ *Example: The tax return preparer has two confirmed allegations of false expenses, deductions, or credits. The treatment is to refer the complaint to the Office of Professional Responsibility.*

4. The case specialist completes a closing checksheet for manager review and approval.

5. The manager reviews and approves the closing checksheet and forwards it along with the complaint package containing the Form 14157 to the CRO clerk.

Management's Response to the Draft Report

July 21, 2014

MEMORANDUM FOR MICHAEL E. MCKENNEY
                DEPUTY INSPECTOR GENERAL FOR AUDIT

FROM: John M. Dalrymple
               Deputy Commissioner for Services and Enforcement

SUBJECT: Reporting Complaints Against Tax Return Preparers – Follow-up
               (Audit # 201340008)

Thank you for undertaking this review of our effort to implement a successful program to address complaints made against paid tax return preparers. Because a majority of taxpayers rely on tax return preparers to assist them in meeting their federal tax filing obligations, it is crucial to identify and address improper preparer behavior in a timely manner. The Return Preparer Office (RPO) is committed to continuously improving the way in which we receive and process return preparer complaints, and we appreciate your assistance with those efforts.

Since the Complaint Referrals office was created in December 2011, we have made significant progress establishing effective processes to handle the large volume of complaints we receive every year. While TIGTA observed a backlog of unprocessed complaints in September 2013, we have since increased staffing, enhanced our processes and written guidance, and trained RPO employees. Further, we are now using a centralized database to manage the complaints. As a result of these improvements, between January and May, 2014, we reduced our inventory backlog by 59%. We will continue to reduce the inventory level and increase efficiencies as we analyze results and refine our processes.

Several conditions in the report involve challenges we have largely overcome. We are confident that if TIGTA were to observe the Complaint Referrals function today, they would find the conditions significantly improved. For example, the risk ranking process no longer relies on the chart in Figure 5. The new risk ranking matrix allows for all complaints to be scored for risk. Also, we no longer use a master spreadsheet to control the work. We recognized that the spreadsheet was a cumbersome tracking method, serving as an initial organizational tool while we worked to get the complaint inventory into a database.

2

As the Complaint Referrals function matures, we will continue to proactively make organizational and process improvements as issues are identified. Our specific comments on your recommendations are attached. If you have any questions, please contact me, or a member of your staff may contact Karen Hunter-Thomas, Director, RPO Strategy & Finance, at (703) 414-2121.

Attachment

Attachment

The Deputy Commissioner for Services and Enforcement should:

Recommendation 1
Establish complaint processing time frame goals that are based on a business case analysis. Once these time frame goals are developed, establish procedures to ensure that the complaints are timely processed.

Corrective Action:
We agree with this recommendation. We are in the process of developing goals that will measure specific components of complaint processing, including timeliness. Developing the goals will be an iterative process over time.

Implementation Date:
September 30, 2015

Responsible Official:
Director, Return Preparer Office

Corrective Action Monitoring Plan
The IRS will monitor this corrective action as part of our internal management system.

Recommendation 2
Ensure adequate separation of duties exists in receipt and recording of complaints into inventory records. In addition, establish a process to periodically reconcile the number of complaints received to the number recorded in the Master Inventory spreadsheet to ensure that all complaints are controlled.

Corrective Action:
We agree with this recommendation. We have already implemented the separation of duties related to receipt and recording of complaints into inventory records. We will also periodically reconcile the number of complaints received to the number recorded in the Return Preparer Database, recognizing that there is no direct correlation between pieces of mail and the number of complaints received.

Implementation Date:
December 15, 2014

Responsible Official:
Director, Return Preparer Office

Corrective Action Monitoring Plan
The IRS will monitor this corrective action as part of our internal management system.

2

Recommendation 3
Ensure that criteria for referring complaints to other IRS business functions are appropriately applied.

Corrective Action
We agree with this recommendation. We now include the IRS business function's point of contact on all referrals so the contact may notify the RPO if the referral criteria were not met. Also, proper application of referral criteria will be addressed during any refresher training, quality reviews, and managerial reviews of complaint processing.

Implementation Date
Completed.

Responsible Official
N/A

Corrective Action Monitoring Plan
N/A

Recommendation 4
Develop a process that accurately tracks complaints that the Complaint Referrals function refers to IRS business functions to ensure that the complaints are received for evaluation. In addition, inventory records should include information as to whether and how the referral was ultimately resolved by the business functions.

Corrective Action
We partially agree with this recommendation. We agree it is important to ensure that all complaints are received by the IRS business function to which they were referred, and have already established an assurance process. We now send all referrals via email requesting confirmation that the email was read. Receipt messages are reconciled periodically with sent items. Unreconciled items are investigated.

We agree that it is important to ensure that referred complaints meet the business functions referral criteria and the inventory records include complaint resolution information. However, rather than tracking the ultimate resolution of each referred complaint, we will instead use the quarterly stakeholder referral meetings as an opportunity to regularly discuss whether referrals were productive and to reassess the continued viability of referral criteria. This will achieve the same result with far fewer of our limited resources than would be required to track every referral.

Implementation Date
Completed

3

Responsible Official
N/A

Corrective Action Monitoring Plan
N/A

Recommendation 5
Ensure that the Complaint Referrals function establishes procedures for case
processors to contact taxpayers for missing information in order to work as many
complaints as possible.

Corrective Action
We disagree with this recommendation. We are focused on reducing the current
backlog of complaints and maintaining currency of complaint processing. Once we
are able to sustain currency and should we have sufficient resources, we will
consider designing a pilot test for contacting complainants who submit incomplete
information as well as an address or telephone number to ascertain the viability and
cost-effectiveness of such contacts. At this time, however, we do not have the
resources to contact complainants or conduct such a pilot.

Implementation Date
N/A

Responsible Official
N/A

Corrective Action Monitoring Plan
N/A

Recommendation 6
Ensure that access to the Correspondence Imaging System (CIS) is provided to
Complaint Referrals function employees to allow them to download electronic copies
of Forms 14157 and related documents.

Corrective Action
We agree with this recommendation. We have already obtained CIS access for our
employees so they may download electronic copies of Forms 14157 and related
documents.

Implementation Date
Completed

4

Responsible Official
N/A

Corrective Action Monitoring Plan
N/A

Recommendation 7
Ensure that the complaint module in the Return Preparer database is updated to
include all data collected on complaints, including the CY 2012 data.

Corrective Action:
We agree with this recommendation and the 2012 complaint data has been
uploaded to the Return Preparer Database.

Implementation Date
Completed

Responsible Official
N/A

Corrective Action Monitoring Plan
N/A

Recommendation 8
Develop the capability to produce management information reports from the
complaint module in the Return Preparer database.

Corrective Action:
We agree with this recommendation. The administrators of the Return Preparer
Database are currently updating the functionality of the database so it may be used
to create management reports.

Implementation Date
June 30, 2015

Responsible Official
Director, Return Preparer Office

Corrective Action Monitoring Plan
The IRS will monitor this corrective action as part of our internal management
system.